Also by Nick Butterworth and Mick Inkpen:

The House on the Rock, The Lost Sheep,
The Two Sons, The Precious Pearl,
The Magpie's Story, The Mouse's Story,
The Fox's Story, The Cat's Story.

Marshall Morgan and Scott
Marshall Pickering
34 – 42 Cleveland Street, London, W1P 5FB, U.K.

Copyright © 1989 Nick Butterworth & Mick Inkpen
First published in 1989 by Marshall Morgan and Scott Publications Ltd
Part of the Marshall Pickering Holdings Group

A subsidiary of the Zondervan Corporation

First published in the USA by
Zondervan Publishing House, 1415 Lake Drive, S.E.,
Grand Rapids, Michigan 49506

British Library CIP Data
Butterworth, Nick
  The rich farmer
  1. Bible. N.T. Parables: Rich fool
  I. Title   II. Inkpen, Mick   III. Series
  226'.8

  cat. # 19106
  ISBN 0–310–55960–X

Printed and bound in Italy

The Rich Farmer

Nick Butterworth and Mick Inkpen

Zondervan Publishing House
Grand Rapids, Michigan

Here is a farmer who is
very rich. The farmer is rich
because his soil is rich.
And his corn grows faster
than anyone else's.

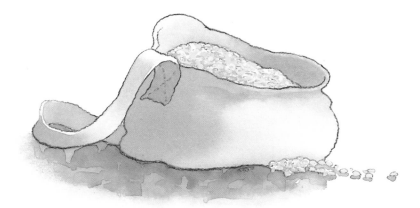

And higher than anyone else's.

And at harvest time he has much more of it than anyone else! Lucky man.

This year he has so much corn that his old barn can't hold it all. It is bursting at the seams.

"No problem," says the farmer. "I will pull it down and build a bigger one. Then next year I will be rich enough to take life easy."

So he builds a bigger barn.

But when harvest comes round
again, the new barn is not big
enough.

The greedy farmer has
planted more corn than before.
And carrots too.

"No problem," says the farmer.
"I will build an even bigger,
better barn. Then next year I
will be richer still and then
I can really enjoy myself."

So he builds a bigger, better
barn.

But at harvest time, even the bigger, better barn is not big enough.

Again the farmer has planted too much corn, too many carrots. (And a few cabbages as well.)

This time, the farmer says to himself. "I will build the biggest, grandest barn the world has ever seen. And then I shall be so rich, I need never work again!"

The barn he builds reaches up to the sky. When it is finished the farmer sighs a great big sigh.

"Tomorrow I will gather in the harvest and then at last I shall begin to enjoy myself. I know! I'll have a party!"

But that very night he dies
in his sleep. Just like that!

The birds eat his corn,
the rabbits dig up his carrots
and his cabbages go to seed.

The big barn stands empty
and the rich farmer never does
get to enjoy his money.

Poor man.

Jesus says, "How silly it is for a man to spend his whole life storing up riches for himself. To God, he is really a poor man."